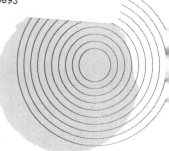

For those with a creative spirit and a thankful heart.

The Creative Gratitude Journal

A 52 Week Daily Gratitude Journal
with Guided Drawing Prompts

Rosanne McBrayer

Using This Journal

1 Everyday you will come up with 3-5 things you are grateful for from the last 24 hours, big or small, and incorporate this list into a mini drawing. Start every list with "I am grateful for..."

2 There are pages that fit 4 drawings and pages that fit 3 drawings. After 7 days, go to the next prompt. The prompt number is on the opposite page.

3 Your words can go around the shapes in your drawing, take the place of part of your drawing, be the blank space around your drawing, be the background under your drawing or frame the drawing.

4 It is recommended that you place a blank piece of paper under the sheet you are drawing on to protect the following page.

Weekly Prompts

1 Plants
Draw the outline of a flowerpot in pencil. Write your gratitude list inside the flowerpot. Erase the pencil lines, leaving the words in the shape of the flowerpot. Draw a plant in the flowerpot.

2 Vines
Draw the branch and leaves of a vine. Write out your gratitude list in the blank space around the branch.

3 Roots
Draw a line 1/3 from the bottom of your drawing space. Under the line, draw roots and write your gratitude list along the roots. Above the line draw a small sprout. Each day, draw that sprout growing larger from the roots you write out.

4 Vases
Write out your gratitude list along the edge of the drawing space. Draw a vase in the center.

Week

1

Week
1

Week
2

Week
2

Week
3

Week
3

Week
4

Week
4

Weekly Prompts

5 Flower Frames
Draw a box inside the drawing space and write your gratitude list inside the box. Outside the box, draw flowers coming out in all directions.

6 Hearts
Each day, draw a heart with a different design inside. Fill the blank space around the heart with your gratitude list.

7 Arrows
Draw an arrow in between each item item on your gratitude list so that your list is in the order of arrow, item, arrow and so on.

8 Dots and Dashes
Write out your gratitude list across your drawing space. Fill the area around the words with designs using dots and dashes.

Week
5

Week
5

Week
6

Week
6

Week
7

Week
7

Week
8

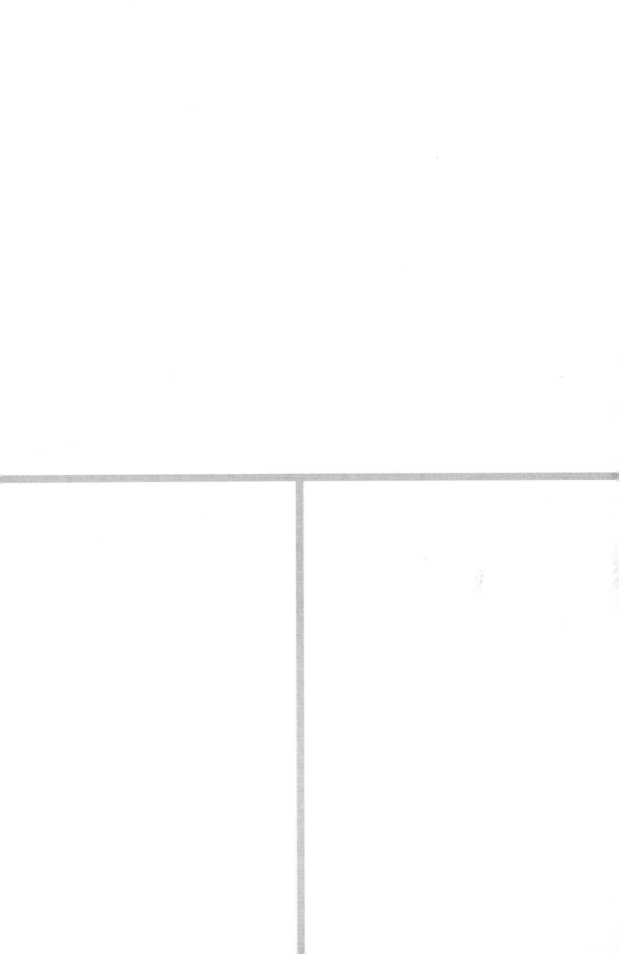

Week
8

Weekly Prompts

9 Triangle Repetition
Draw a triangle and repeat that shape as a pattern. Add as many other shapes as you like. Write your gratitude list in the design.

10 Circles
Draw a circle. Write your gratitude list around the circle. Using only lines and circles, make a design inside the circle.

11 Crystals and Rocks
Draw crystals or rocks jutting out from any side of your drawing space. Write your gratitude list in the center.

12 Geometric Frame
Draw a shape with four or more sides along the edge of your drawing space. Repeat the shape 2-4 more times at a slightly different angle. Write out your gratitude list inside the frame.

Week
9

Week
9

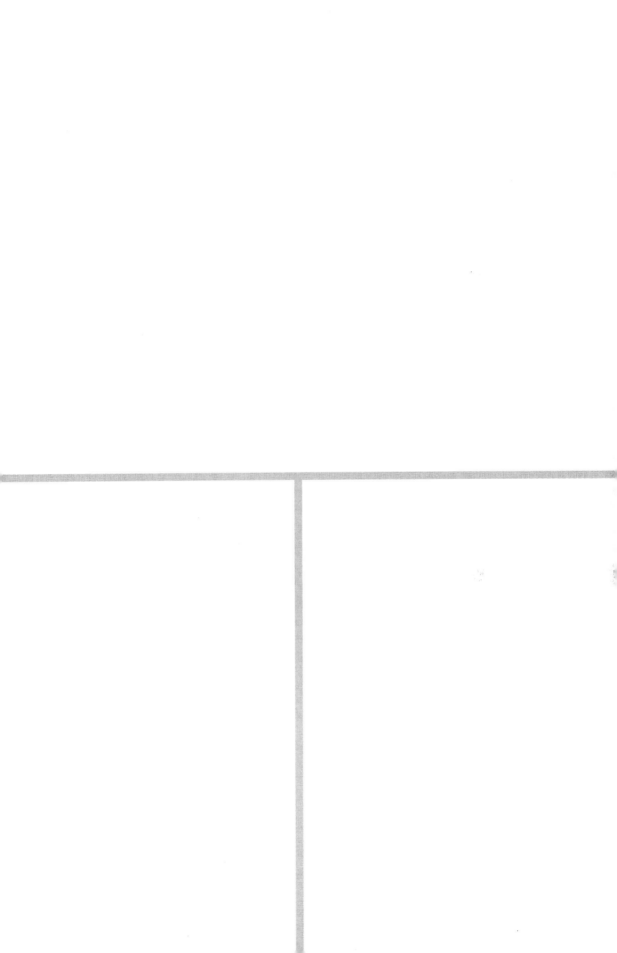

week
10

Week
10

Week
11

Week
11

Week
12

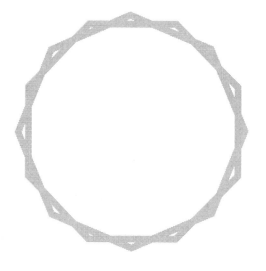

Week
12

Weekly Prompts

13 Flowers
Draw a flower. Write your gratitude list along the flower petals.

14 Bouquets
Write your gratitude list around the edge of the drawing space. Draw a flower bouquet in the center.

15 Birds
Draw a bird. Write your gratitude list in the blank space around the bird.

16 Webs
Draw a spiderweb that fills up the drawing space. Write your gratitude list in the blank spaces between threads in the web.

Week
13

Week
13

Week
14

Week
14

Week
15

Week
15

Week
16

Week
16

Weekly Prompts

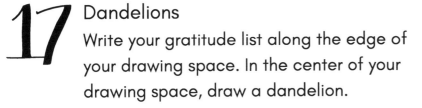

17 Dandelions
Write your gratitude list along the edge of your drawing space. In the center of your drawing space, draw a dandelion.

18 Grasses
Draw a line 3/4 down in your drawing space. Write your gratitude list under the line. Above the line, draw grass growing upward.

19 Butterflies
Write your gratitude list across the drawing space. Over the list, color in or draw a butterfly.

20 Honeycomb
Draw a design by repeating a hexagon honeycomb shape along the edges of your drawing space. In the center, write your gratitude list.

Week
17

Week
17

Week 18

Week
18

Week
19

Week
19

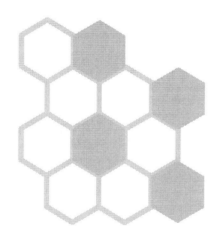

Week
20

Week
20

Weekly Prompts

21 Seashells
Draw a seashell. Write your list in a circle around the shell.

22 Waves
Draw an ocean wave. Write your gratitude list along the curves of the wave.

23 Palm Fronds
Write your gratitude list across the drawing space. Over the the list, draw or color in a palm frond.

24 Tropical Flowers
Write out your gratitude list along the edge of your drawing space. Draw a tropical flower in the center.

Week
21

Week
21

Week
22

Week
22

Week
23

Week
23

Week
24

Week
24

Weekly Prompts

25 Mountains
Draw mountains along the bottom edge of your drawing space. Write your gratitude list above the mountains.

26 Clouds
Draw a cloud in pencil. Write your list inside the cloud. Erase the pencil leaving the list in the shape of the cloud. Add more clouds in the rest of the space.

27 Trees
Draw trees in the center of your drawing space. Write your gratitude list below the trees.

28 Leaves
Write out your gratitude list across the drawing space. Over the list, draw or color in a leaf.

Week
25

Week
25

Week
26

Week 26

Week
27

Week
27

Week
28

Week
28

Weekly Prompts

29 Cactus
Draw a cactus. Write your list in the blank space around your cactus.

30 Succulents
Draw a succulent. Write your list in a circle around the succulent.

31 Feathers
Draw feathers along the top of your drawing space. Write your gratitude list below the feathers.

32 Dream Catchers
Write out your gratitude list along the edge of your drawing space. Draw a dream catcher in the center.

Week
29

Week
29

Week
30

week
30

Week
31

Week
31

Week
32

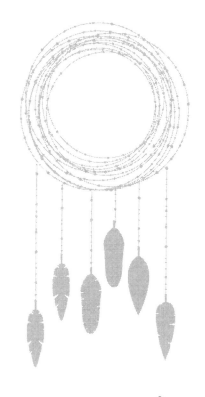

Week
32

Weekly Prompts

33 Confetti
Write your gratitude list across the drawing
space. Over the list, draw confetti.

34 Beverages
Draw a beverage. Write your gratitude list in
the blank space around the drink.

35 Cakes
Write your gratitude list along the edges of the
drawing space. Draw a cake in the center.

36 Houses
Write out your gratitude list along the bottom of
the drawing space. Above the list, draw a house.

Week
33

Week
33

Week
34

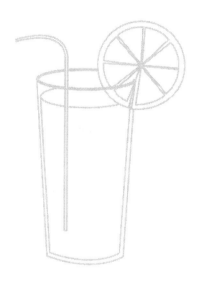

Week
34

Week
35

Week
35

Week
36

Week
36

Weekly Prompts

37 Stars
Draw a star with any number of sides. Write your gratitude list inside the star.

38 Constellations
Write your gratitude list along the edge of the drawing space. Draw a constellation in the center.

39 Moon
Draw a moon. Write your gratitude list along the curve of the moon.

40 Galaxy
Write your gratitude list in the center of the drawing space. Draw any kind of celestial shape around your gratitude list.

Week
37

Week
37

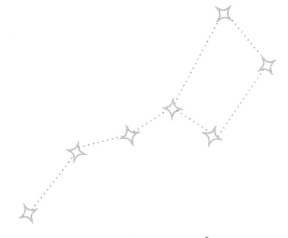

Week
38

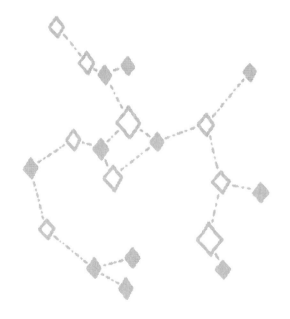

Week
38

Week
39

Week
39

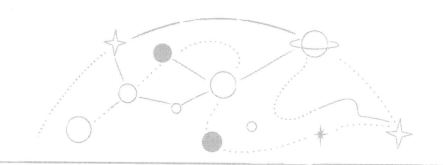

Week
40

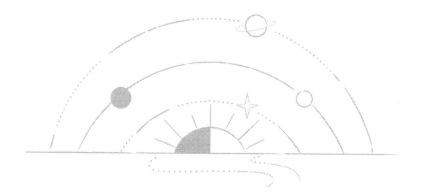

Week
40

Weekly Prompts

41 Mandalas
Draw a circle that fills up the drawing space.
Draw smaller circles centered within the
larger circle. In between the circles, write out
your gratitude list. In the blank spaces left,
draw a repeating pattern.

42 Sunbursts
Write your list across the drawing space. Over
the list, draw a sunburst design.

43 DIY Pattern
Start on one edge or corner of the drawing
space and make a pattern. Repeat the pattern
half way up the drawing space. Write your
gratitude list in the empty half.

44 Skyline
Write your gratitude list along the bottom of the
drawing space. Above it draw a city skyline.

Week
41

Week
41

Week
42

Week
42

Week
43

Week
43

Week
44

Week
44

Weekly Prompts

45 Doodle Frames
Draw a box and add doodles inside the box.
Write your gratitude list outside the box.

46 Scribble
Write your gratitude list across the drawing
space. Draw a scribble line over the list. Add
more scribble lines that intersect the first line.
Draw a pattern or color in each of the resulting
shapes.

47 Mazes
Draw a maze. Write your gratitude list in the
maze.

48 Stream
Draw a stream winding through your drawing
space. Write your gratitude list along the stream.

Week
45

Week
45

Week
46

Week
46

Week
47

Week
47

Week
48

Week
48

Weekly Prompts

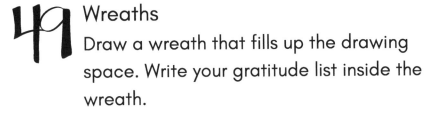

49 Wreaths
Draw a wreath that fills up the drawing space. Write your gratitude list inside the wreath.

50 Garland
Draw strings of garland across your drawing space. Write your gratitude list along the sways of your garland.

51 Ornaments
Draw ornaments along the top of your drawing space. Write your gratitude list under the ornaments.

52 Snowflakes
Draw a snowflake. Write out your gratitude list in the blank space around the snowflake.

Week
49

Week
49

Week
50

Week
50

Week
51

Week
51

Week
52

Week
52

Made in the USA
Columbia, SC
30 December 2019